The Story of

presents

the world premiere

of

UNICORNS, ALMOST

by

Owen Sheers

directed by

John Retallack

First performed in Hay-on-Wye
on 24 May 2018

www.unicornsalmost.com
#unicornsalmost

UNICORNS, ALMOST
Owen Sheers

Keith Douglas **Dan Krikler**

Director **John Retallack**
Designer **Lucy Hall**
Assistant Designer **Luned Gwar Evans**
Sound Designer **Jon Nicholls**
Producer **Emma Balch**

Blind Bookworms Jazz Band
is supported by
Ronnie Scott's Charitable Foundation

The performance lasts approximately one hour.

There will be no interval.

There will be no admittance or re-admittance
while the performance is in progress.

*Please be mindful that in this intimate performance space,
any noise such as rustling programmes, talking, or the ringing
of mobile phones will cause distractions.*

Biographies

DAN KRIKLER | ACTOR

Following his training at Laine Theatre, Arts Dan performed in a number of West End shows, including *Loserville*, *Mamma Mia!* and *Jersey Boys*. In 2016 he completed an MA at Central School of Speech and Drama. Upon graduation he was cast as the lead character, Arthur, in the Bristol Old Vic UK tour of Owen Sheers's *Pink Mist*, a role for which he received widespread critical acclaim in the national and regional press.

OWEN SHEERS | WRITER

Owen Sheers is a poet, novelist and playwright. Twice winner of the Wales Book of the Year, his books of poetry include *Skirrid Hill*, winner of a Somerset Maugham Award, and the verse drama *Pink Mist*, winner of the Hay Festival Poetry Medal. In 2018 he was awarded the Wilfred Owen Poetry Award. Owen's theatrical work includes *The Two Worlds of Charlie F.*, winner of the Amnesty International Freedom of Expression Award, *Mametz*, and National Theatre Wales's seventy-two-hour *The Passion*. Chair of Wales PEN Cymru and Professor in Creativity at Swansea University, he lives in the Black Mountains of Wales with his wife and two daughters.

JOHN RETALLACK | DIRECTOR

John Retallack has been a theatre director for over thirty years. His production of *Pink Mist* by Owen Sheers toured the UK in Spring 2017, after sustained runs at Bristol Old Vic and the Bush Theatre in London. He was the founding Artistic Director of Actors Touring Company/ATC London (1977–85), Artistic Director of Oldham Coliseum (1985–88) Artistic Director of the Oxford Stage Company at the Oxford Playhouse (1989–99), and founding Artistic Director of the new writing company, Company of Angels (2000–2010). From 2010 to 2013 he was Associate Director at Bristol Old Vic where he remains an Associate Artist. He has been a guest director of productions in America, Japan, India, Portugal, Belgium, Austria, Holland and Ireland. All of his companies have toured internationally and John's work has been seen all over the world.

Production Acknowledgments

Thank you to
Ronnie Scott's Charitable Foundation
for funding the Blind Bookworms Jazz Band
project led by Sam Obigbesan, Rachel Starritt
and Eleanor Wait, and supported by
the Royal National College for the Blind.

The graphic identity for *Unicorns, Almost*
was created by Nick Bell.

The limited edition sheet of the Keith Douglas poem,
'Simplify Me When I'm Dead', was designed
and printed from metal type by **Incline Press.**

Thanks also to:

Faber & Faber, Desmond Graham, Hay Festival,
Leeds University Library Special Collections,
Old Forest Arts, The Poetry Bookshop,
The Swan at Hay, Rosco Paints, Whaleys of Bradford

Owen Sheers would like to thank
Emma Balch for her undying enthusiasm
and energy in making this production possible,
Lucy Hall for her design, John Retallack
for his directorial vision, Jon Nicholls
for creating Douglas's world in sound
and Dan Krikler for his talent and dedication
in embodying the man and the poet on stage.

At 20, Castle Street in Hay-on-Wye
we have an exhibition and bookshop
for *Unicorns, Almost.*

Please see **www.thestoryofbooks.com**
for opening times and updates on special events.

THE STORY OF
BOOKS

WHERE STORIES ARE TOLD AND BOOKS ARE MADE

The Story of Books
is an initiative to create a dynamic
working museum that celebrates
the ongoing story of books.
Through collaboration with experts
and enthusiasts, **The Story of Books**
creates meaningful experiences
where stories are told and books are made.

Contact info:

The Story of Books,
Baskerville Hall,
Clyro, HR3 5SB

info@thestoryofbooks.com
Emma Balch: 07879 373431

www.thestoryofbooks.com
where stories are told and books are made

Twitter **@thestoryofbooks**
Instagram **@thestoryofbookshq**
Facebook **@tellingstoriesmakingbooks**

#thestoryofbooks

Introduction

While on tour with Owen Sheers' play *Pink Mist*, which I
directed for the Bristol Old Vic, Owen introduced me to the
work of Keith Douglas. I was fascinated by his 1944 memoir
From Alamein to Zem Zem and also by his extraordinary
poems. I found it hard to believe that Douglas had died at the
age of only twenty-four – his writing is already so rich and
accomplished.

Then, when I watched Owen's BBC Four documentary on Keith
Douglas, I began to see how passionately Owen felt about this
poet – though I should have realised before when, over a drink,
Owen recited 'Simplify Me When I'm Dead' from memory. This
play is from one poet and about another. And it insists that the
poems be acknowledged for what they are – the most original
to emerge from World War Two.

Despite that originality Douglas's work was largely ignored in
the wake of the war. In 1961 his mother went into her local
bookshop in Kent, where Douglas was brought up, to find all
six copies of the original publication of his poems still on the
shelf, untouched, unread. That publication would, though, be
essential to the survival of his poetry, enabling future writers
and critics such as William Scammell and Ted Hughes to
discover Douglas's writing and begin to bring it back to the
world's attention.

The Story of Books is intent on bringing the essential nature of
print and printing to life for a wider public. Hence, everyone
who attends a performance of the play will receive a printed
copy of 'Simplify Me When I'm Dead'. This play is an apt first
outing for this innovative long-term project.

Owen and I are especially thrilled that Dan Krikler is playing the
role of Keith Douglas. Dan played the leading role of Arthur on
the national tour of *Pink Mist* and we are delighted that he is
available for the three-week run of the play here in Hay-on-Wye.

Owen has single-handedly done so much to ensure that
Douglas is not forgotten. We hope that you enjoy watching
today's performance as much as we have in rediscovering this
brilliant young poet of 1944.

John Retallack, Director
April 2018

Unicorns, Almost

Owen Sheers is a poet, novelist and playwright. Twice winner of the Wales Book of the Year, his books of poetry include *Skirrid Hill*, winner of a Somerset Maugham Award, the verse drama *Pink Mist* winner of the Hay Festival Poetry Medal and the BAFTA-nominated film-poem, *The Green Hollow*. In 2018 he was awarded the Wilfred Owen Poetry Award. Owen's theatrical work includes *The Two Worlds of Charlie F.*, winner of the Amnesty International Freedom of Expression Award, *Mametz* and National Theatre Wales's seventy-two-hour *The Passion*. Chair of Wales PEN Cymru and Professor in Creativity at Swansea University, he lives in the Black Mountains of Wales with his wife and two daughters.

OWEN SHEERS

Unicorns, Almost

FABER & FABER

First published in 2018
by Faber and Faber Limited
74–77 Great Russell Street,
London WC1B 3DA

Typeset by Country Setting, Kingsdown, Kent CT14 8ES
Printed and bound by CPI Group (UK) Ltd, Croydon CR0 4YY

A CIP record for this book
is available from the British Library

ISBN 978-0-571-23188-1

2 4 6 8 10 9 7 5 3 1

Acknowledgements

This play is partly an adaptation of Keith Douglas's memoir *Alamein to Zem Zem* and his letters. I am grateful to the Keith Douglas estate for permission to quote from these works. Desmond Graham's biography of Douglas has been an invaluable resource, as have Desmond's personal insights into Douglas, the man and the poet. I am also grateful to Josie Rourke, Kate Pakenham and The Old Vic where this play was originally developed, and to the Hay Festival for hosting an early reading with Joseph Fiennes.

Introduction

To render a lived life on stage can, at times, feel like an imposition; the shaping and patterning of the dramatist smoothing out a character's rough edges in places and magnifying them in others. Not every life is suited to theatrical telling, nor every voice fitted to such a space. To bring Keith Douglas into dramatic being, however, has never felt anything other than natural: as a poet, a soldier, a son and a lover, he feels born for the stage.

Why is that? There is, undoubtedly, a strong theatrical frame of reference in his work, especially in his memoir of the fighting in the Western Desert, *Alamein to Zem Zem*. The battlefield is 'a stage', the dead, and their 'props' 'crawling off at a queer angle to the scenery'. There is, too, something of the actor's self-awareness in Douglas's writing about himself, in this memoir and in his letters. Douglas died young (at the age of twenty-four) and like all young people he spent much of his early years of adulthood trying on a succession of fronts, masks, poses. He is always the lead role in his own production. When the war enters this story it brings with it an even stronger note of self-awareness together with a darker timbre of dramatic tension. Suddenly, as in a play, the final curtain feels ever-present: the resonance of an imminent end shadowing the immediate action.

For me, though, it is the quality of Douglas's poetic voice that, ultimately, makes his transition from the page to the stage feel so organic. Douglas, across the handful of poems he wrote in what was, under the pressure of war, an accelerated education as a poet (as with Wilfred Owen before him in thr First World War), becomes a master of the direct address. 'Look,' he says to us again and again, deploying a talent for acute reportage distilled into poetry. 'Look at this and *see*.' More than most poets there is a quality to his register, his approach, that makes a reader feel they are being spoken to personally – singled out of the audience and asked to lean closer to the footlights. There is, too, a dramatic immediacy to his line and the movement of his poetry. 'Like a piece of ice on a hot stove,' Robert Frost once said, 'a poem should ride on its own melting.' That is what Douglas achieves with the best of his work: a natural and spontaneous release of observation, thought, rhythm and feeling.

It is this quality of immediacy that Ted Hughes returns to again and again when writing a letter about Douglas to William Scammell.

> For me the question that circumscribes all my thoughts about Douglas is – how did he manage to make such final and in their way archetypal and manifestly indestructible designs sound so spontaneous, so much like the thought of a moment? . . . It's that imprint of intimate presence – a naked activism of a very essential, irreducible self . . . a unique sort of essence, spiritual and hard to come by. Less talent, or facility, than a quality of being.

Hughes and his introduction to the Faber edition of Douglas's *Complete Poems* was vitally influential in bringing Douglas's poetry to attention. Reading this letter, you can't help but wonder if Douglas wasn't equally influential in the forming of Hughes's own poetic voice. I've often thought, for example, that the first appearance of Hughes's 'Thought Fox' might be glimpsed in a line from Douglas's 'The Offensive': 'the mind, mobile as a fox / goes about the sleepers waiting for their wounds.'

'The thought of the moment'. 'A quality of being'. These are the poetic qualities I hope an audience will experience in witnessing Douglas and his poems resurrected on stage. I hope, too, that they will sense what I think is essential in any one-person play – namely a forceful pressure to speak. In Douglas this pressure is twofold, both personal and societal. Personally there is the fact that his poems, for which he sacrificed so much and for which he made an almost Faustian pact with the war, are today far from well known or well read. He desperately wanted his poems in print not because of any authorial vanity but rather, I have always felt, because he knew that the sand in his glass was fast running out and that those few poems would, in effect, be his only chance of outliving his life.

The second pressure to speak is that which informs the opening scene of this play, based upon real events when Douglas was home on leave. He asks us to 'look' in his poems so that we will truly see what war is, and in that seeing make a genuine attempt to bring an end to one of humanity's most persistent failures – the resorting to violent conflict as a means of solving our disputes. Enter Douglas into the twenty-first century, a century in which we can, if we choose, see further and clearer than ever before. And yet here we are, still doing it.

In one of his last poems, 'Actors Waiting in the Wings of Europe' (there's that theatrical reference again) Douglas leaves the unfinished draft on the following line,

> There is an excitement
> in seeing our ghosts wandering

I hope, in conjuring Douglas to the stage and having him haunt that space for an hour or so, an audience will feel a similar excitement – the voltage of live theatre infused with the presence of a gifted poet embodying before us the melancholy admixture of his too-brief journey into eloquence.

Owen Sheers, April 2018

Unicorns, Almost was first performed in Hay-on-Wye, Powys, Wales, on 24 May 2018, produced by The Story of Books.

Keith Douglas Dan Krikler

Director John Retallack
Designer Lucy Hall
Assistant Designer Luned Gwar Evans
Sound Designer Jon Nicholls
Producer Emma Balch

Blind Bookworms Jazz Band, supported by Ronnie Scott's Charitable Foundation

UNICORNS, ALMOST

Blackout.

The sound of an old film projector. A Pathé newsreel plays across and through a gauze. A dogfight: a British and German plane wheeling about each other. A burst of gunfire and the German plane spins out of the sky, trailing a plume of smoke.

The sound of an audience clapping and cheering.

Keith Douglas stands from the front row and turns to face the audience.

At first he is inaudible, but soon he is shouting.

Keith You shits! You bloody stupid shits! You stupid, stupid shits!

He backs away towards the screen as if evading stewards.

You stupid bloody fools!

Blackout.

Radio static rises with the lights. Keith Douglas is standing upstage. As he approaches the audience the static tunes between fragments of broadcast speech and music.

Music: 'It Ain't Necessarily So' by Gershwin.

I'll make a bloody mark on this war, that's what I said . . .

Military Intercom . . . *I'm just going over Beecher's myself . . .*

Radio Announcer . . . *One poet who fought against Hitler who can lay a claim to greatness is Keith Douglas.*

(*Sung.*)
   'Yukon Jake was tough as a steak,
   Hardboiled as a picnic egg . . .'

Milena . . . *He had this trick. He'd ask me to scribble on a piece of paper . . .*

Radio News Announcer . . . *On July 4th Rommel's forces broke through to Tobruk . . .*

Keith . . . My dear Mother, we are beginning to look like heroes already . . .

Mother . . . *He was always interested in language . . .*

Keith . . . I don't know if you have come across the term 'bullshit' . . .

Colonel . . . *Yes, prickly chap, effeminate . . .*

Keith (*spoken not shouted*) . . . You fools, you bloody stupid fools . . .

As he reaches the front of the stage the static reaches a pitch, then tunes into silence.

He is wearing a basic Second World War desert military uniform: long trousers, shirt, ingrained with sand, smeared with oil. He is tall, thin, mid-twenties, with a moustache. He wears a pair of glasses which he removes and cleans. Putting them back on, he looks out at the audience.

Silence.

Keith The most impressive thing about the dead is their silence.

Proof against anything in the world.

I saw them all the time in the desert – the unburied corpses, littering the ground everywhere.

German, Italian, British, Australian.

All of them lying around like day-trippers taken ill.

Theatrical dummies holding impossible poses.

Until the gases inside them heated up, of course.

Then they'd go wriggling off, crawling at a queer angle to the scenery.

The sun turns their faces crisp black.

But so silent.

It's a strange thing to us who live, isn't it? Silence, I mean.

We desire it, we fear it, we worship it, we hate it.

I mean look at me. Still talking.

You might not think it but the view from a moving tank is a lesson in silence.

The engine drowns everything, so for me, it was like looking out on a silent film.

Men shout, vehicles move, planes fly over, all soundlessly.

For hours on end.

I was 'destined' for the tanks, I suppose.

The cavalry were always my favourite you see, even when I played with my lead soldiers as a boy.

They seemed so much more . . . dramatic.

The charging Highlanders with their kilts and plumes flying out behind them.

Often in the wrong direction – their heads would break off and I'd fix them back on with matches so they tended to swivel easily . . .

I played at soldiers a lot as a boy. I was an only child but I had a vivid imagination – a sheet over a couple of old chairs at the bottom of the garden was all I needed to be commanding whole battalions of imaginary troops.

My mother would come home some days and find me guarding the gate in puttees, cap and a threepenny medal pinned to my chest.

I was eight years old.

I didn't get to play at the real cavalry stuff until much later.

I'd been in the cadets at school, but it was at Oxford, in the horsed regiment of the OTC, that I finally got to imitate those charging Highlanders.

I wasn't that good actually.

I didn't have my own horse for one thing, unlike most of the others.

But I was keen, very keen.

As I was when I eventually joined up, when the war began at the start of my second year.

He snaps to attention and salutes.

'Cadet Douglas reporting for duty. Sir!'

Softening my boots every night with the back of a toothbrush.

Practising my cuts and thrusts with my new chromium-plated sword.

Silly really, playing with a sword when Spitfires and Messerschmitts were dogfighting overhead.

I loved the horses though. So . . . ancient.

The smell of them, drying in a stable.

Can you believe that cavalry horses aren't allowed to shit on the floor?

We had to 'guard' against it. Whip out a shovel at the appropriate moment.

At least there was none of that when we switched to the tanks.

Our instructor said we'd come to love our tanks as much as we'd loved our horses.

I'm not sure that was ever true.

Tanks let you down a lot.

Or at least the lazy bastards back in engineering let you down a lot.

And a horse will never become your coffin.

Or an oven, roasting you.

Beat.

For all its fighting talk it's surprising how efficient the army can be at keeping a man out of the action.

I had to steal a truck in the end. To get to the war.

Our regiment might have modernised from horses to tanks but when I arrived in Egypt in June of '41 I soon realised most of the officers hadn't made the same leap.

Yes, they were climbing into the turrets of Grants and Crusaders, but they may as well have still been mounting thoroughbreds and hunters.

Real 'Old Boys'. Jodhpurs, riding crops, that kind of thing. Landed gentry – brought half their estates with them and treated the rest of us like tenant farmers.

My colonel, Piccadilly Jim, was one of these original 'horsed' officers, as they called themselves.

I didn't quite see eye-to-eye with him.

Which is probably why when the rest of my regiment went off to the front I found myself in Alexandria stuck in a camouflage job back at Divisional HQ.

Playing in sandpits with toy tanks – climbing up stepladders to look at them through the wrong end of a telescope.

Not my idea of a war.

So I took the truck.

My batman was impressed, at least.

'I like you, sir,' he said. 'You're shit or bust you are.'

> *The thump of distant artillery.*
>
> *Faint radio reports of Alamein rise under his speech.*

I'd heard the battle of Alamein begin from Alexandria.

The thumping of the guns along the western horizon.

And now here I was, just a few days later, driving into it in my stolen truck through the whole arrangement of the army, too large to appreciate.

As a body might look to a germ riding in its bloodstream.

Vehicles everywhere, lorries appearing like ships, plunging their bows into drifts, rearing over crests like waves. Every man wearing a white mask of dust.

Their eyes, when they take their goggles off, look like clowns' eyes.

Most of us keep our goggles on though, and handkerchiefs tied like a cowboy's over our mouths.

It's impossible to breathe if you don't.

There are so many trucks, tanks, cars, lorries that the sand is pulverised into liquid.

Step in it and your leg sinks to the knee.

I've been in Egypt for over a year by now but this is the first time I've seen any of this.

Which is, of course, why I'm here.

The battlefield, you see, is the stage of war. And the desert is the most perfect stage of all.

No towns, no civilians, just two armies, facing each other over the sands.

It's here on the battlefield where things happen.

It's here men kill and are killed. Here where we endure hardships and here, oddly enough, where we are moved to a feeling of comradeship with the enemy – with the same men who kill us and who we kill.

Simply because we're all living in the same unnatural, dangerous, but not wholly terrible world.

It's fascinating to see.

There was nothing back in Alexandria to excite a poet or a doctor or a painter.

But here . . . well, here, it's a new world.

Beat.

When I eventually find my regiment among all this confusion Piccadilly Jim is pleased to see me, which is a relief.

I had thought he might send me packing, in which case I intended to drive on to Palestine and amuse myself at the nearest harem until I was captured and court-martialled.

But no, he was fine with me turning up.

Most of the other officers in A-Squadron had already been killed, so he was happy to get whatever reinforcements he could.

'Good evening, sir,' I said. 'I've escaped from division for the moment, so I wondered if I'd be of any use to you up here.'

'Well, Keith,' he said. 'Out for a duck again?'

He smiles.

'Out for a duck.' A cricket term. Of course.

Bowled out before you've even made a mark on the scoreboard.

That evening I'm shown to my tanks.

Three Crusaders, low-built, squatting like toads in the dark.

I meet my crew. Evans the gunner, Welsh, hardly ever says a word, and Moodie the driver, Glaswegian, never shuts up. Except in battle.

Wakes up talking, like a bird.

I unpack my equipment into the turret and catch the smell of cologne.

The last officer must have been in here just this morning.

It's impossibly cramped inside. Barely room for the three of us.

Rows and rows of shells lined around the sides, resting on their wasp-coloured noses.

We lie down to sleep under the stars. The whole regiment at an hour's notice to move, and for the first time I find myself assuming I will die tomorrow.

When I took the truck that morning, as I was driving out into the desert I'd felt a weight lift from me. As if I'd put down a heavy box.

I suppose I'd been more ashamed than I'd realised. Of my safe job back at HQ.

But now, lying in the dark beside my tanks, that lightness has become something sharper, and I realise I've not only exchanged a vague and general existence for a more simple one, but also quite possibly a shorter one too.

> Tonight's a moonlit cup
> and holds the liquid time
> that will run out in flame,
> in poison we shall sup.
>
> The moon's at home in a passion
> of foreboding. Her lord
> the martial sun, abroad
> this month will see Time fashion

the design we begin:
and Time will cage again
the devils we let run
whether we lose or win . . .

So in conjecture stands
my starlit body. The mind
mobile as a fox goes round
the sleepers waiting for their wounds.

This overture of quiet
is a minute to think on
the quiet like a curtain
when the piece is complete.

I'm not going to try and describe what that first battle was like.

Or what the months of fighting that followed it were like.

There's no point. It's almost impossible to convey – that impression of having walked through the looking-glass that touches a man on entering a battle.

But I will tell you some of the things I learnt after I drove that truck into the desert.

After I went looking for the war.

That battle can be more beautiful than you'd expect.

The different colours of shells and tracer fire at night for example.

Arcs of reds and yellows, from us to them, from them to us.

That the cargo of a solitary silver bomber unloaded in the sun looks like an isolated shower of rain.

That moments of intense fear can transform into moments of exhilaration at the blink of an eye.

That dogs don't discriminate between German, British, Italian or Libyan corpses.

That the clothes on a dead body often have an instinct for decency, wrapping themselves around the places where arms, legs or heads should be.

That our tanks rarely last for more than three days before they break down.

That the wrong drugs will be put in our morphine syringes.

That my trousers will fall round my ankles because the buttons saw themselves off.

That there's a rare satisfaction in brewing up with your crew during a gap in the shelling.

That looting will become one of our greatest pleasures.

That the loot we gather will reveal everything the Germans have is better than ours.

That the Italians will booby-trap boxes of wine, and dead bodies.

That a killed corporal's blood spilt in the turret will jam up the workings of the machine gun.

That in time, the flies will bother you more than the shells.

That before this I never actually knew what tanks *looked like* in action – that not one film or newspaper report or training manoeuvre comes close to describing the chaos.

That after a month's fighting I'm able to pick up an oily copy of *Esquire* in the middle of battle and flick through its pictures, looking at the pink Petty Girl and the white smiles of the Hollywood stars while the shells scream overhead.

That shells never scream.

That they sound more like someone tearing cloth . . . or like an express train . . . or like someone whispering into a microphone . . . or . . .

He whispers.

'Out for a duck again, Douglas?'

He pauses, transported by his own line of thought.

Have you ever seen someone, suddenly, in the street, on the train, on the bus, and known, immediately that you want them?

You've never seen them before, but something about them convinces you that they'll complete you, in every way.

Make you the person you were always meant to be.

Maybe you catch their eye, you glance at each other, but then they're gone.

They're off the train, off the bus, someone else, some damn fool, has moved between you and them and when they move again, that person has gone and the vacuum they leave is filled with what-ifs. Maybes.

You might have seen them for no more than a couple of seconds, and yet their face can stay with you for a lifetime.

A ghost that haunts you, maybe until your dying day.

Some of you are thinking about them right now, aren't you?

That man, that woman you saw last week, last year, ten years ago.

The one you never spoke to, the one you never reached out for.

Well, I didn't want to live with what-ifs. Maybes.

So when I saw Milena walk past – her easy stride, the long muscles in her calves working against the sand – I went after her immediately.

This was in Alexandria, on Stanley Beach, which was always thick with beauties.

As was the whole city.

I know people say you can't beat English girls but I'm telling you for sheer beauty any Egyptian, Syrian or Arab girl knocks them into a cocked hat.

Their appearance is quite ordinary in Alex but they'd make the occupants gasp of any room they entered back home.

I don't drink or smoke nearly as much as the other officers but there's only so long one can go without the third indulgence, so yes, I do 'explore' while I'm in Cairo and Alex.

Olga, Latvian.

Then Fortunee, Iraqi . . . Renée, French Jewess.

Reman, Turk.

Marcelle, Turkish

Pilar, Spanish. Lovely hands.

And then, walking past on Stanley Beach, Milena. Spanish Italian.

I catch up with her, we talk and I ask her out for a drink that night.

She says yes.

Six weeks later I ask her to be my wife.

Again, she says yes.

It's amazing, isn't it?

How the weight of one person added to your life can tilt it, until its edges catch the sun.

With Milena, I was quite happy to stay in Alex.

Quite happy to carry on looking at model tanks through the wrong end of a telescope in my stupid, dull job at HQ.

The city became our playground.

Tea at the Cecil Hotel, then dinner and dancing at the Monseigneur, or cocktails at the Metropole, if we have the money.

When we don't, a slow ouzo in a café on the Boulevard Saad Zaghoul.

Dinner at her parents' house, where everyone talks at once and I can't understand any of them.

Long, slow afternoons in bed.

Sometimes I'd ask her to scribble with a pencil on a blank piece of paper.

Then I'd take it. Add a line here, some shading there, a dot here and as if by magic a scene appears.

A market. Two lovers in a crowd.

There'd always be a scene in there somewhere.

There always is.

When we dance she moves beside me like a velvet curtain in the wind.

He begins to dance with an imaginary woman.

Her body is sinuous and cleanly made.

Like a drawing made with an airbrush.

A face of delicate bones. Like the hollow bones of a bird.

A nobility of line.

A twisted smile and curious, sad, dishonest eyes . . .

He drops his imaginary partner.

Norman Illet was my best friend at school.

We went up to Oxford together too.

He joined the navy and now he'd turned up in Alex as brown and ridiculously muscular as ever.

Sometimes all three of us go out together, me, Milena and Norman.

To the beach. For drinks. Swimming at the Pyramids.

One night I'm on the way out to HQ when my truck breaks down in the desert.

I tow it back into the city and go to Milena's house.

Norman's there.

Milena and I go upstairs to find some blankets and that's when she tells me.

She hasn't even told Norman yet.

I don't stay.

I was twenty-two when this happened.

Milena was my fourth engagement. Not a great track record, is it?

Ying Chen was my first. At Oxford. Daughter to the Chinese ambassador to Washington.

Not bad for a scholarship boy from Kent wouldn't you say?

She used to come to my rooms and I'd draw her. She liked that.

We bought a little red sports car together.

I drove her back to my old school in it once. Even made her wear an oriental dress.

Just in case anyone missed the point.

She was out of my class, though, or at least, I wasn't of hers.

It was Ying Chen who introduced me to Antoinette. No doubt to get me off her back.

Well, it worked. For a while. But then I bitched that up too.

So when I sail for Egypt it's Diana, sweet sixteen, who's waving a handkerchief from the quayside.

I suppose I wanted someone to get my widow's pension.

Beat.

That probably sounds rather cynical, doesn't it?

Well, you mustn't mistake me. I'm never cynical when it comes to making love.

If I tell you between two kisses, for example, that I love you, you can believe me.

But not for long.

Love comes in waves.

It can't be kept burning at the same pitch forever or it'll burn you up altogether.

Sometimes, when I was sleeping with Ying Chen she'd say, at a moment when I'm sure I should have been mad with emotion, 'My God, how I love you.'

And I'd think, 'My God, how affected that sounds.'

It was like I was watching a film and all the time thinking about how I'd tell Norman about it when I got home.

Norman.

Milena understood love I think.

I remember thinking as I walked home that night, that this is how a man must feel when he has to walk for miles with a bad wound.

Dragging his feet so as not to feel the wound too much.

I wrote a very bad poem about it all.

He 'quotes' his own poem, playing up the juvenile drama. The poem, however, gets the better of him in the end.

I listen to the desert wind
that will not blow her from my mind;
the stars will not put down a hand,
the moon's ignorant of my wound . . .

. . . Like a bird my sleepless eye
skims the sands who now deny
the violent heat they have by day
as she denies her former way.

All the elements agree
with her, to have no sympathy
for my impertinent misery
as wonderful and hard as she.

O turn in the dark bed again
and give to him what once was mine
and I'll turn as you turn
and kiss my swarthy mistress pain.

Beat.

It's a couple of weeks after that night at Milena's that I take the truck and drive out to the front line.

Milena, meanwhile, is still in Alex, as beautiful as ever and, I think, happy, if only I'll leave her alone.

It's less than a day's driving to the front, no more than forty miles, but at the end of it the cafés and beaches of Alex are much further away than that and everything is strange again.

The fighting is vicious. My first relief is that I bear up, I cope.

My second is that at times I even enjoy myself.

Once we've driven the Germans off their line it's then a matter of chasing after them as they retreat across the desert.

The enemy remain mostly unseen. Their shells arrive among us, randomly killing. Their tracer fire rakes our camps at night, but often that's it.

We only ever get close to them when they capture us or we capture them.

When a party of prisoners march past I set my jaw and glower at them through my goggles, doing my best to look like part of an unstoppable war machine.

One day my sergeant catches a boy who's been sniping at us while we're brewing up.

He can't be more than fourteen. Eyes hard as marbles.

The sergeant's all for 'shooting the little bugger now'.

But we don't. Not this time anyway.

As we advance we pass through the aftermath of our own battles.

Vehicles are scattered everywhere, squashed flat or still entire, stunned like beetles.

At other times we'll stop and find ourselves in a sudden paradise, a thick carpet of blue-green desert flowers undulating into the distance.

33

Their sweet smell is so strong it even reaches me in the
turret, overpowering the stench of machinery and oil.

Nothing ever quite covers the smell of the dead though,
who also lie around everywhere, like actors at the end of
a tragedy.

The props of their last performances are often littered
about them.

A holed water bottle; a bloody, fly-covered towel.

Two Italians caught in a clumsy embrace in the turret of
their tank, like twin embryos in a womb.

More than once I find myself close enough to look one
of them in the eye, and when I do, his silent gaze holds
mine like that of the Ancient Mariner's, speaking of
another land, far away and yet so near.

Just over the horizon, perhaps no more than a minute
away.

> Three weeks gone and the combatants gone
> returning over the nightmare ground
> we found the place again, and found
> the soldier sprawling in the sun.
>
> The frowning barrel of his gun
> overshadowing. As we came on
> that day, he hit my tank with one
> like the entry of a demon.
>
> Look. Here in the gunpit spoil
> the dishonoured picture of his girl
> who has put: *Steffi. Vergissmeinnicht*
> in a copybook gothic script.
>
> We see him almost with content,
> abased, and seeming to have paid

34

and mocked at by his equipment
that's hard and good when he's decayed.

But she would weep to see today
how on his skin the swart flies move:
the dust upon the paper eye
and the burst stomach like a cave.

For here the lover and killer are mingled
who had one body and one heart.
And death who had the soldier singled
has done the lover mortal hurt.

*Radio static and intercom communications rise
through faint static.*

King 2 (*voice over*) *'King 2, now that chap's retired to
the pavilion how many short of a full team are you?
Over.'*

Douglas gives a wry smile.

King 1 (*voice over*) *'King 1, someone's throwing stones
from the edge of the boundary. Can't see from where
yet. Over.'*

Static.

Keith Cricket.

This is how we talk about the battles raging outside our
turrets.

The terms come from the 'Old Boys', of course, but we
all end up using them.

Static.

King 2 (*voice over*) *'King 2, just going out to bat now.
Over.'*

35

Static.

Keith Once, during a rare moment of silence, I get into awful trouble for interrupting this 'commentary'.

He 'joins in' the radio communications.

'Now there seems to have finally been a tea break at Lord's, can someone please get on to that 88 on my left? Over.'

Radio static and further radio communications.

Tom (*voice over*) *'Uncle Tom, what's the going like over this next bit? Can we bring the unshod horses over it? Over.'*

Static.

Keith Horses. That's the other main source of allusion at Alamein.

Cricket and horses.

Static.

Tom (*voice over*) *'Uncle Tom, I'm just going over Beecher's myself. You want to hold 'em in a for bit but then it's good going for the whole field. Over.'*

Static.

King 2 (*voice over*) *'King 2, slow down a bit, Uncle Tom, and have a good look from hull down before you go swanning over the fences, will you? Over.'*

Static.

Keith Now Tom's an interesting one.

The only officer who's got a foot in every camp, fits in with the Old Boys, the odds and sods like me, and with the men.

He's got what he calls the 'gift of the blarney' which helps.

More importantly though, he's been a stable lad, a jockey and a horse dealer before the war.

Sold horses to the colonel's estate . . .

Static.

Tom (*voice over*) *'Uncle Tom, having a bit of trouble with my horses' insides. Can we have the vet? Over.'*

Keith 'translates' the radio communications while also telling Tom's story.

Keith His crankshaft's gone – again. They need the mechanic.

Tom married at twenty-one.

Now, ten years later he's got two daughters.

He showed me a photo of the youngest once. Already as bandy-legged as her father.

'Ridden at Olympia,' he tells me.

He was very proud of that. Very proud.

Static.

Tom (*voice over*) *'Uncle Tom. My horse has cast a shoe. Can we have the farrier? Over.'*

Static.

Keith Now his track's come off. He's stuck up there, on the ridge.

Silhouetted against the skyline. A perfect target.

It's like watching an inexperienced tightrope walker.

Waiting.

Tom rode professionally, first over the sticks and then on the flat.

He seems to have met every famous face in racing.

By the end of his first day he also knows the name of every man in his company.

I think I was jealous of Tom.

His easy manner.

Piccadilly Jim thought the sun shone out his arse.

> *Radio static . . . but no speech.*

Every now and then a more hesitating transmission creates a short silence.

> *A communication comes over. A different voice.*

Nuts 3 *'Er, Nuts 3 calling. We 'ave, er, 'ad a misfortune. Horse has fallen. Jockey's no more. Can we have monkey orange?'*

Keith What he means is their tank's been hit, Tom's been beheaded and the driver's bleeding from a great wound.

Can they please have monkey orange – the Medical Officer – because the tank is on fire. Their faces are swelling into unrecognisable yellow vegetables.

Eyes without lashes.

Huge mouths dribbling and moaning like children
exhausted with crying.

They are burning to death.

Over.

*He segues into another poem, at first read with a
restrained anger. But again, as he moves through the
stanzas, the words transport him into a more tender
register.*

The noble horse with courage in his eye,
clean in the bone, looks up at a shellburst:
away fly the images of the shires
but he puts the pipe back in his mouth.

Peter was unfortunately killed by an 88:
it took his leg away, he died in the ambulance.
I saw him crawling on the sand; he said,
'It's most unfair, they've shot my foot off.'

How can I live among this gentle
obsolescent breed of heroes, and not weep?
Unicorns, almost,
for they are fading into two legends
in which their stupidity and chivalry
are celebrated. Each, fool and hero, will be an immortal.

These plains were their cricket pitch
and in the mountains the tremendous drop fences
brought down some of the runners. Here then
under the stones and earth they dispose themselves,
I think with their famous unconcern.
It is not gunfire I hear, but a hunting horn.

Silence.

It helps to keep things at arm's length.

Talking like that. The cricket and horses.

Takes away the *meaning*.

'Advance', 'Retreat', 'Bowled out', 'Lost a shoe', 'Objective reached'.

The words become unfaithful on the tongue.

Which is just how we like it, thank you very much.

Looking through the wrong end of the telescope.

My problem is that poetry, good poetry anyway, should turn that telescope back the right way round.

Bring it all up close.

Too close for comfort perhaps, for some.

All of us write, of course.

The men, the Old Boys, Tom.

To wives, lovers, mothers, children.

And they write back.

Thousands of letters tracking us across the desert.

Essential as any supply line.

As an officer I spend much of my downtime censoring these letters.

Removing whatever gets close to *meaning* anything.

Most are depressingly formulaic anyway. Starting 'Well dear' or 'Well pal', according to sex and ending all too often in a galaxy of Xs.

Orders are to erase these Xs. To blank out the kisses.

Could be a code and we can't have Jerry seeing that, can we?

I don't though. I add a few more instead.

That way any code is buggered and lucky Lucy back home just thinks her Tommy loves her more than ever.

My own correspondence is left alone.

There are never any Xs anyway.

Wouldn't be appropriate really, signing off to T. S. Eliot at Faber's with sloppy kisses . . .

The whole time I'm in the desert I manage to stay in touch with the literary world back home.

A fragile thread of letters keeps me in the loop.

My mother, god bless her, sends me periodicals and new publications.

She also sends my stuff out to magazines. And to Mr Eliot.

He's kind enough, 'Promising young poet, please send more,' that kind of thing.

Can't help wondering what I'd get for his autograph . . .

That's where the poets and editors are, you see. Back home.

Or behind the front, at a desk. In London, Oxford.

Writing beautiful verse with the odd oblique reference to a bomb.

There are none, it seems, who actually live with the fighting troops.

No one like Owen or Sassoon in the last war.

There were no poets at Dunkirk for example.

Or if there were, they stayed there.

Who knows? Perhaps we didn't need any after all.

I mean, hell can't be let loose twice, can it?

It was let loose once in the Great War and it's the same old hell now.

The same behaviour of the living.

The same appearance of the dead.

I see the poems of Rosenberg, Owen, Sassoon, illustrated on the battlefields of the Western Desert every day.

So perhaps there *is* nothing new to say.

Just silence.

I carry drafts and drafts of my poems around with me.

Stuffed into the pockets of my battledress.

They don't come easily you see.

It's the precision that takes time. The tuning.

Some of the poets back home don't agree.

John Hall, for example, a good friend, writes from the London Arts Club.

Says I'm losing my 'musicality'.

Getting too distant. Or too close. Whichever, certainly too hard.

I reply.

He 'reads' the letter, acknowledging the irony of the opening address:

'Dear John,

'You say I fail as a poet, when you mean I fail as a lyricist. I am surprised you should still expect me to produce musical verse. I don't know if you have come across the word bullshit – it's an army word and signifies humbug and unnecessary detail. It symbolises what I think must be got rid of – the mass of irrelevancies, of "attitudes", "approaches" . . .

'To write on the themes which have been concerning me lately in lyrical and abstract forms, would be immense bullshitting.

'In my early poems I wrote lyrically, as an innocent, because I was an innocent: I have (not surprisingly) fallen from that particular grace since then. I won't disagree with you when you say I'm awkward and not used to the new paces yet. But my object (and I don't give a damn about my duty as a poet) is to write true things, significant things in words each of which works for its place in the line.

'I see no reason to be musical about things at present. When I do, I shall be so again, and glad to.'

Now in my dial of glass appears
the soldier who is going to die.
He smiles, and moves about in ways
his mother knows, habits of his.
The wires touch his face: I cry
NOW. Death like a familiar, hears

and look, has made a man of dust
of a man of flesh. This sorcery
I do. Being damned, I am amused
to see the centre of love diffused
and the waves of love travel into vacancy.
How easy it is to make a ghost.

The weightless mosquito touches
her tiny shadow on the stone,
and with how like, infinite

a lightness, man and shadow meet.
They fuse. A shadow is a man
when the mosquito death approaches.

Beat.

Are you superstitious?

Do you see *meanings* in things? Signs?

I'm not sure I do.

God knows, I felt lucky to survive out there for so long, unharmed.

But that was all. Lucky.

So I'm surprised, when it finally happens, to remember a horoscope written for me when I was thirteen years old.

We're chasing the enemy towards Tripoli.

The whole squadron is caught in a shallow depression.

Shell bursts everywhere.

Sitting ducks.

My Crusader's hit, clean through the turret. I feel the shell miss my stomach by inches.

Later I find myself stranded. Exhausted.

Running and walking over open ground under the watchful eye of a German tank.

I wait for him to fire. The hail of bullets. But he doesn't.

I want him to. Anything other than capture.

To be honest I'm flapping a fair bit.

Thinking over and over about how I mustn't be captured.

I come across a corporeal from C Squadron.

His right leg ends in a tattered brush of bone and flesh.

So then I have to carry him too. His good leg and his stump under each arm.

His hands locked at my throat.

The German gunner watches. Just watches.

Eventually we find some scout cars. I bundle him into one of them and it's as I'm walking to the other that I step through the trip wire.

The mine explodes behind me. I'm still standing.

Then a second one goes off and I topple forward, sprawled on the sand.

Like a day-tripper, taken ill.

Ten years after that horoscope was written for me in a shabby fairground tent in Tunbridge Wells I find myself jolting along in a hospital train back towards Alex with shrapnel wounds spattered up my 'spine, legs, calves and ankles'.

It's my twenty-third birthday.

A man beside me keeps up a steady chant all the way.

'Oh, I didn't want to fight, didn't want to fight.

Had a good job, had a good job, didn't want to fight, didn't want to fight.'

I can't join in, although God knows it hurts enough.

I mean, I had wanted to fight, hadn't I? I took the truck.

Came looking for all this.

And I suppose now I've got what I came for.

Experience. The other side of the looking-glass.

A glimpse through the right end of the telescope.

A notebook full of sketches and drafts of poems.

I take all of it away with me in that hospital train, all the way to Number One General Hospital El Ballah in Palestine, where, lying on crisp sheets, sitting in the sun, I write it all down.

True things. In words each of which works for its place in the line.

That's all.

That, I thought, would be enough.

I was in hospital for six weeks. A wound in my foot is slow to heal.

I'm soon able to walk though.

On my first day out I sit down at a café in Tel Aviv, open the paper and read of Piccadilly Jim's death.

He was killed standing up in his turret, shaving apparently.

I do eventually return to the regiment, but it's hardly recognisable.

Most of the old faces have gone.

And the campaign's over pretty soon anyway.

Only the newest reinforcements pose for the press, dirty and torn like battle-worn heroes.

Those of us who actually fought the campaign manage to keep clean on half a cup of water a day.

After a period of leave we're ordered to remove cap badges and flashes, which can mean only one thing.

We're going home.

It's over. After the months of fighting, of keeping on the move, it's finally over.

I for one, however, hope to be back. Once the war's done.

I like Egypt. A cushy job here with the British Council. Or in Palestine.

Something like that.

I've no desire to stay still after this.

And no desire for England at all.

Beat.

It's a strange homecoming because we all know we're not really coming home.

It might be over in the desert, but the war's still there.

They'll be opening the second front in Europe soon.

Britain is a waiting room. Full of Yanks, Canadians and us, all of us waiting.

No one knows when it'll happen. When we'll be thrown back into it.

Just that we will.

When I walk down Oxford Street under the Christmas lights I can't help wondering if I'll still be here to see them again next year.

I take the opportunity of three weeks' leave to visit my mother in East Grinstead.

She's keeping house there for a Colonel Barber and his wife.

It's like being back in my schooldays. Holidays spent at someone else's house.

Always someone else's house.

Or rented rooms.

   Beat.

My mother fell ill when I was very young – no more than four, five years old?

'Sleepy sickness' was how my grandfather explained it to me. *Encephalitis lethargica.*

I preferred 'sleepy sickness', though. Has the ring of a fairy tale about it, doesn't it?

All we needed was the handsome prince, and she'd be right as rain.

I remember seeing her carried out on a stretcher. Then they took her away.

Someone I'd never met before led me up to my room and locked the door on me.

I beat against it. Screaming. Shouting every curse I'd ever heard.

'Cursedamnbotherdarnbloody!'

Hitting my head again and again against the door knob.

Well, that bloody hurt, so I stopped doing that and just fell to crying instead.

It was no good though. They'd all gone. The house was silent.

So silent.

It was my grandfather who came for me in the end.

And that's when he told me.

'Sleepy sickness.'

Very common after the First War apparently.

As was my father's condition I suppose.

I wonder what the Latin name for *that* is?

He'd done well in the army. Bit of a hero actually.

Won the MC at Gallipoli, wounded at Diala.

The first time I ever remember seeing him was in this role.

The returning hero.

Jumping from the dinner table to burst into song, holding a chair above his head with one arm.

> *He sings.*

> 'Yukon Jake was tough as a steak,
> Hardboiled as a picnic egg.
> He combed his hair with the leg of a chair
> and drank his beer by the keg.'

I think my father must have enjoyed the army.

The war was good to him in a way.

It was the peace afterwards that got to him.

He left when I was eight.

With Olwen, who helped with our housekeeping.

He never came back.

So much for the handsome prince.

So that's why the rented rooms.

The holidays in other people's houses.

That's why it's always been just me and Mother.

Her moving from position to position, from house to house, and me, a rather poor replacement for the handsome prince, dropping in at the end of each term.

Or, like now, at the end of each campaign.

She seems more settled this time. At least, more than usual.

She's pleased to see me in one piece I suppose.

Apparently Egypt's left me with a 'more mature and relaxed manner'.

She seems happy.

So I feel fine about leaving her for a bit and going on to Oxford and London.

I have a lot to do you see.

A lot to sort out before it all starts again.

Because I know that it will, even if I don't know when.

Time gets squeezed between those two thoughts, between that knowledge and that ignorance.

Compressed, like a fine ore between two strata of rock, until it's so thin there's nothing you can do to stop it slipping through your fingers.

Can you imagine what that's like?

Living with a totally different idea of time to those around you.

That's why I work so hard on the poems.

I must seem an awful bore.

A friend of mine, Joan Appleton, runs a club for allied servicemen in Oxford.

She invites me to visit her there, and when I do I spend all my time scribbling away in the back room while she serves tea out front.

She asks me to give a talk on my desert experiences.

So I do. I tell them all about it.

The sudden expanses of desert flowers.

Her scents, her moods, the dawn light across her sand dunes.

I'm sure Joan expected heroics. *Boys' Own* adventure stories.

But these men haven't seen action yet.

They'll be plenty of time for that later I tell her.

I'm not sure she understands.

I'm not sure if anyone can, if they haven't been there.

Which is why I find Tambi so bloody frustrating.

My dear mother has been sending him my poems the whole time I'm in Egypt and now, as editor of *Poetry London*, he's agreed to publish both a memoir of the desert fighting and a collection of my poems.

He offers me sixty pounds for the memoir and a measly ten pounds for the poetry.

But that seems to be as far as it gets.

Tambimuttu, I learn, is a hard man to pin down.

I try to talk to him in his office when I'm in town, but that's easier said than done.

He appears to be on a mission to single-handedly keep the pubs of Fitzrovia afloat during these difficult times.

Him and his gaggle of young poets.

Oh, I don't doubt he's serious about the work. He is.

But at the same time his bi-monthly *Poetry London* hasn't appeared for the last *twelve* months, which does make me somewhat nervous.

I'm terrified he's going to lose the only copies of the manuscripts I have.

And he certainly doesn't share my view of time.

Has no idea of how accelerated my world has become.

I can't seem to make him understand that although this is my first collection of poems, it's also quite possibly my life's work.

It's soon already too late.

I'm ordered back to the regiment, back to a camp of tin huts in a sea of mud that freezes every night.

Back to inspections, to the metallic smell of the turret.

To censoring letters.

To waiting.

Spring comes on like a symphonic accompaniment to a Sam Goldwyn hit.

I'm made a captain and given 119 men to look after.

One day I order four of them to go and pick primroses for the huts.

Much to their blushing embarrassment.

We begin training in Shermans over 'European' terrain.

Fitting inflatable skirts to the tanks.

It's started again.

He slips into the poem.

And all my endeavours are unlucky explorers
come back, abandoning the expedition;
the specimens, the lilies of my ambition
still spring in their climate, still unpicked:
but time, time is all I lacked
to find them, as the great collectors before me.

The next month, then, is a window
and with a crash I'll split the glass.
Behind it stands one I must kiss,
person of love or death
a person or a wraith,
I fear what I shall find.

Beat.

Tambi might not be able to give me the assurances I'd
like about my books, but he does, without knowing it,
give me something else.

Or rather someone else.

Betty is Tambi's assistant. More or less holds the office
together.

She's already read my poems. A calling card of sorts,
I suppose.

She's a bit older than me. Brittle and beautiful. Defensive.

Which makes her moments of giving all the more
magical.

The refugee of a crumbling marriage.

And no, before you ask, it wasn't me who shook the
foundations.

But I am there to pick up the pieces.

Betty goes riding once a week in Hyde Park.

On my last day of leave she arranges a horse for me too.

I take her dancing at the Piccadilly afterwards, then at sparrow's fart the next morning, I catch the train back to camp.

I don't think Betty has any idea the difference that last dance made.

He laughs at himself.

I find myself writing to her as soon as I get there, like a boy returning to school from the holidays.

It's a queer relationship.

Betty has something of a 'cat's cradle' of a life.

I can't quite make the equation work out. But I like that.

Lots of unknowns.

We make plans to sail the world together after the war and when I can I breach the camp security to catch a night with her up in town.

She rots me up a lot when I say I won't survive the invasion.

Once, as I'm leaving, she looks at me in that challenging way of hers and says, 'You're my *bête noire*, you are.'

Bête noire. The black beast.

She always did have a knack for putting her finger on it.

Hitting the mark.

Now she's named it, this personal monster of mine, brought it out into the open, I can't avoid trying the poem.

I can't though.

I can draw it. Black care sitting behind a horseman.

A medieval animal with a dog's face.

But I can't write it.

I try for five hours.

He fires through one of his attempts.

The beast is a jailer
allows me out on parole
breaks into my conversation . . .
if this is a game it's past half time and the beast
   is winning.

He breaks off.

I have sensations of physical combat trying to write this.

I can see his tracks in all my other poems. Anyone can.

But he won't come. It won't work.

He gives another burst of his attempts.

The trumpet man to take it away
blows a hot break in a beautiful way
ought to snap my fingers and tap my toes
but I sit at my table and nobody knows
I've got a beast on my back.

Suppose we dance, suppose we run away
into the street, or the underground

he'd come with us. It's his day.
Don't kiss me. Don't put your arm round
and touch the beast on my back.

He breaks off again, dissatisfied. Beat.

55

Bête Noire then is the title of my first collection and also the title of the poem I can't write.

A protracted failure, which is also a protracted success I suppose, because it is, after all, the poem I start to write in all my other poems.

> *He gives a final burst of this 'failure' but slows,*
> *changes down a gear, towards the last line.*

> If at times my eyes are lenses
> through which the brain explores
> constellations of feeling,
> my ears yielding like swinging doors
> admit princes to the corridors
> into the mind, do not envy me.
> I have a beast on my back.

> *Beat.*

We know the time is near when we start training with amphibious tanks.

We're moved to a secure camp.

No one in, no one out.

I do manage one last night with Betty though.

I persuade her to book a hotel room with me.

Just so I don't have to fight against all of London for every moment with her.

So we can shut the door on all our problems. Just for an hour.

Just for long enough to know that what we have is more than a brief mirage.

I tell her to keep writing to me. Above all, keep writing.

To assume I'm alive unless she hears otherwise.

I tell her I think I can fight on through anything if there's only her to look forward to at the end of it all.

I hate fighting. Make no mistake of that.

I'm played out as a soldier. My head swivels too easily . . .

I suppose I could get out of it if I really wanted to.

But I don't see why my friends should get blown up while I drop out.

And anyway, I'd asked for this, hadn't I? I took that truck.

Went looking for the war.

So perhaps it's only fair it should come looking for me now.

And even if I did stay behind, it would only make me feel worse than going, I know that for sure.

But I'm not fighting *for* anything. Certainly not for England.

Any country that can treat its soldiers like skivvies the way England does can go to hell for all I care.

No, it's just a case of fighting *against* the Nazis now.

Which has to be done I suppose. Which is fine.

As long as we all know what that means.

Beat.

A year or so after I joined up I went to the cinema, in Oxford one night.

The usual Pathé newsreel was showing before the main feature.

Two planes in a dogfight.

The German plane's hit. Goes spinning to the ground, pluming black smoke.

The audience cheer. And clap. They applaud its fine pirouette.

They applaud the war.

All they can see is the plane.

They don't see the pilot, fumbling with his belt.

The man, screaming.

The telegram, dropping to the doormat.

His wife reading it.

The silence after the crying.

They don't see any of this.

Just the plane going down.

The film has brought the war to them. Right before their eyes.

And they don't see a bloody thing.

Beat.

I'm sure I was the last person Skinner expected to see standing at the back of the church.

It was the evening before the invasion.

He'd gone to evensong in Sway. We were stationed nearby, on the coast.

A few hours before he'd held his own service beside my tank.

A couple of upturned ammo crates for an altar. Folded blankets for kneelers.

But now he'd come to attend one himself.

We were the only two men in uniform in the whole congregation.

Afterwards he suggested a walk.

He was a good padre, Skinner.

Could probably tell I was a bit out of sorts.

So we walked and talked. All night.

Through the New Forest. Along the lanes.

I'm sure I confused him a good deal.

Telling him of my plans for after the war one minute, then asking him to send a nice letter to my mother the next.

He was very kind. Told me not to be so silly.

Was sensible enough not to get all godly on me either.

A brave man too.

I fished him out of the water as we landed.

He'd got stranded somehow, trying to get the wounded out of the sinking tanks.

Because it did finally happen.

Those two thoughts, that knowledge and that ignorance, they finally met, squeezing out time altogether until suddenly there we all were, in the moment, waiting for hours on the pitching landing craft, the decks awash with vomit, a force five gale and salt spray stinging our faces.

Waiting for when the whole armada, all five thousand vessels

would begin throbbing their way over to France.

I'd managed to get a last letter off to Betty.

I'm not sure it made much sense – the typical mix of sickly sentiment and embarrassed bravado, something of a hallmark in those weeks leading up to it all.

'Dear Betty,

'I only hope you loved me yesterday as much as I loved you, whatever happens.

'DON'T say "Thank you for your incredibly sentimental letter", because I've said it for you, and anyway, I should come to London leave or no leave and spit in your eye.

'All my love, Keith.

'PS. I wish I'd kissed you goodbye properly – shyness again.'

Beat.

And so we wait.

Six tanks to a landing craft, rocking on our moorings, everything soaking wet and the knots in our stomachs tightening by the hour.

Actors waiting in the wings of Europe
we already watch the lights on the stage
and listen to the colossal overture begin.
For us entering at the height of the din
it will be hard to hear our thoughts, hard to gauge
how much our conduct owes to fear or fury.

Everyone, I suppose, will use these minutes
to look back, to hear music and recall
what we were doing and saying that year
during our last few months as people, near
the sucking mouth of the day that swallowed us all
into the stomach of a war. Now we are in it

and no more people . . .
There is an excitement
in seeing our ghosts wandering.

Beat.

The view at dawn is truly extraordinary.

Ships and boats stretching into the distance as far as we can see in every direction.

France appears through the mist and spray. A dark smear on the horizon.

Two of our squadrons have to 'swim' on to the beach,

flopping their amphibious tanks into the sea half a mile from shore.

They have the worst of it.

Some of them sink immediately.

Others are rammed and sunk by our own craft.

My squadron's luckier. We land right on to the beach.

By the time we get there it's already a mess of shattered and burning vehicles.

I see Skinner in the water, fish him out and carry on up towards the German defences.

And I'm fine.

The Germans are on the run.

We continue inland, impeded more by the traffic than by any fearful counter-attack.

We do meet resistance. Snipers. Heavy machine-gun fire.

But I survive.

That night we sleep outside the village of Bayeux.

Under the stars again.

It's a few days later it happens. Outside St Pierre.

I'm running down a ditch with Bethell-Fox, another officer.

Reporting back on a division of Jerries we've spotted over the river.

A mortar shell explodes in a tree above me.

Skinner hears about it that night, but the CO won't let him forward to recover my body.

Somehow he makes his way to the spot the next day though, and when he gets there he's surprised to find I'm completely unmarked.

Not a mark anywhere.

He buries me under the hedge. Reads the order of service under sporadic rifle fire.

A few days later the regiment passes the same spot again and there are my boots, sticking up through the mud.

There'd been a lot of rain.

Heavy rain.

Skinner did write to my mother.

And I suppose Betty must have carried on writing to me for a while. Until they told her.

My book of poems was eventually published. In 1951.

Not by Tambi of course.

And not as *Bête Noire* either. My *Collected Poems*, no less.

Ten years after they came out my mother went into her local bookshop to find all six copies of the original order still on the shelf.

I had hoped that through them I might stick around for her in some way.

'Live on' in the words and all that.

But no, they were still there. Unread.

Untouched.

Not a mark on them.

Not a mark anywhere.

Just silence.

   Beat.

   Remember me when I am dead
   and simplify me when I'm dead.

   As the processes of earth
   strip off the colour and the skin
   take the brown hair and blue eye

   and leave me simpler than at birth
   when hairless I came howling in
   as the moon came in the cold sky.

   Of my skeleton perhaps
   so stripped, a learned man will say
   'He was of such a type and intelligence,' no more.

   Thus when in a year collapse
   particular memories, you may
   deduce, from the long pain I bore

   the opinions I held, who was my foe
   and what I left, even my appearance,
   but incidents will be no guide.

   Time's wrong-way telescope will show
   a minute man ten years hence
   and by distance simplified.

   Through that lens see if I seem
   substance or nothing: of the world
   deserving mention or charitable oblivion

not by momentary spleen
or love into decision hurled
leisurely arrive at an opinion.

Remember me when I am dead
and simplify me when I'm dead.

Fade to black.

Rising radio static segues between snatches of 'It Ain't Necessarily So' by Gershwin, before fading again, to silence.